Make sure you are sitting properly at your desk.

Hold your pencil lightly. You should hold it about three centimetres from the point.

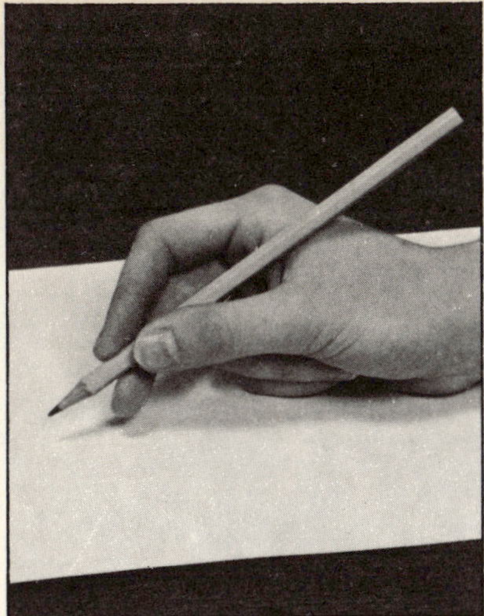

Let your pencil point along your arm.

 Practise these exercises many times until you can do them lightly, smoothly and quickly:

Straight lines

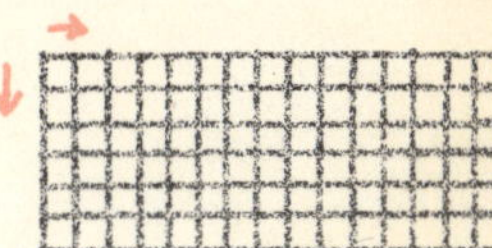

Saw teeth

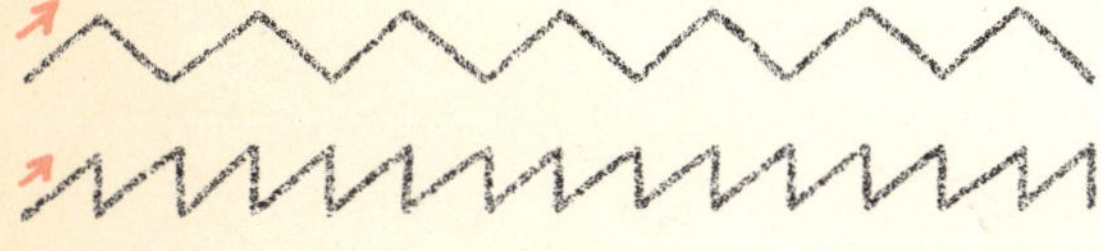

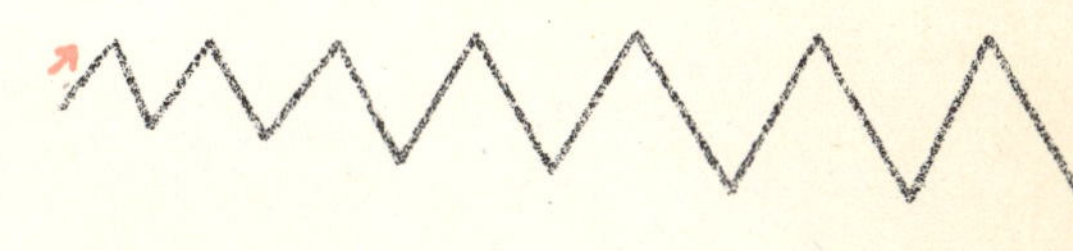

Curves

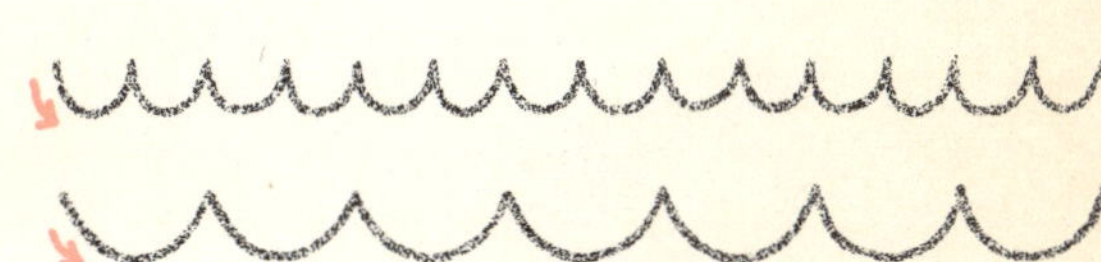

Ovals and spirals

In Book 1 you learned how to make all the letters and joins but you will need revision to be sure you make all letters and numerals correctly.

Study each set of letters below in turn then close the book and write out that set from memory. Check that you got them all right. Repeat this exercise until you can write out the whole set from memory, correctly, quickly and well.

Lower case letters

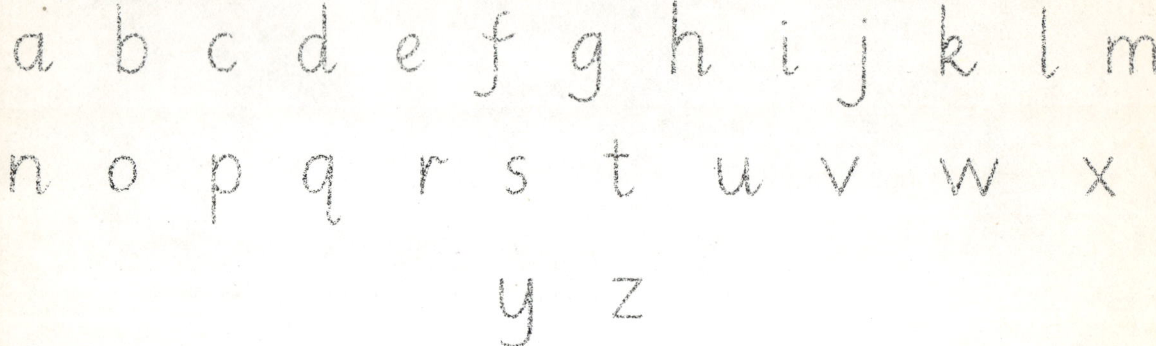

Capital letters

Numerals

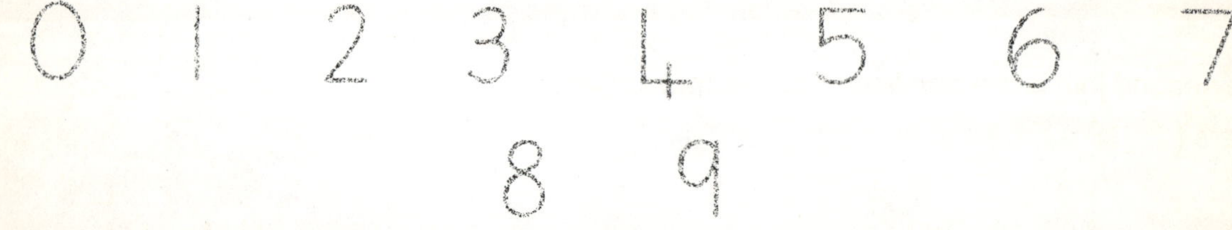

The basic join is the one made from the end of a Set 1 letter to the beginning of a Set 2 letter. The join is the same as the up-swing in the swings pattern.

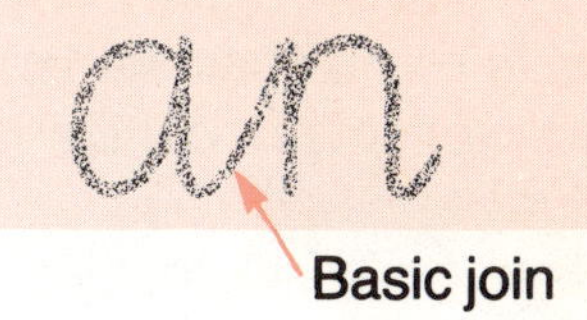

Basic join

Set 1 letters are a c d e h i k l m n t u

Set 2 letters are a c d e g i j m n o p q r s u v w x y

Practise the swings pattern:

uuuuuuuuuuuuuuuuuuuuuu

Practise these words:

can cup day din ham
him land man mat tap

Pay special attention to joins to e and s

came canes deeds dine
heads lend manes men

The second join is the one from Set 1 letters to Set 3 letters (b f h k l t).

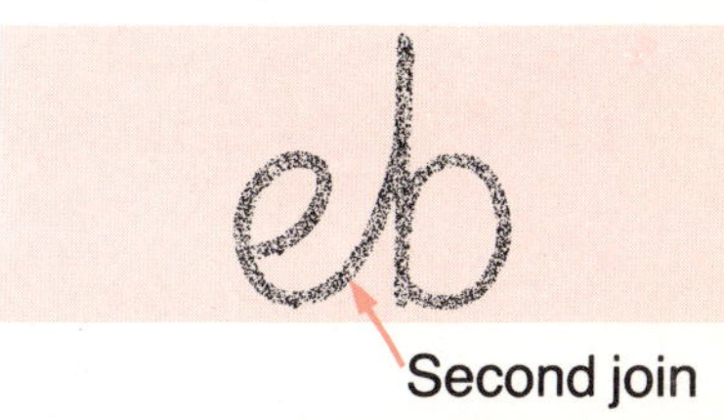

Second join

cake club deck bath after

The third join is the one made from the Set 4 letters (f o r v w) to Set 2 letters. Remember the join is a shallow horizontal curve. Keep the space between letters constant.

Third join

Practise these words:

arrow barn coin face

from moon rope wife

Pay special attention to the joins to e and s:

bars cliffs fence hose we

have laws rent toe

The fourth join is made from Set 4 letters to Set 3 letters (b f h k l t).

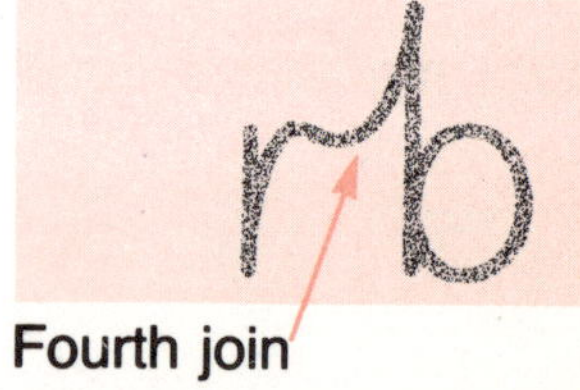

Fourth join

book flower heart hole

robe sofa shot work write

The break letters are the ones after which no join is made (b g j p q s x y z).

box gas globe jam pest

The Lion Pride

A family of lions is called a pride. There are usually about ten lions in a pride. Female lions are called lionesses. The babies are called cubs.

Lions roar to tell other lions where they are. They are lazy and often sleep all day.

Lions live in Africa and India.

Bengal

There once was a man of Bengal
Who was asked to a fancy dress
ball;
He murmured "I'll risk it,
and go as a biscuit ....."
But a dog ate him up in the
hall.

ANONYMOUS

The Worm

Today I saw a little worm,
Wriggling on his belly,
Perhaps he'd like to come inside,
And see what's on the telly.

SPIKE MILLIGAN

The Crocodile

How doth the little crocodile
Improve his shining tail,
And pour the waters of the
Nile
On every golden scale!

How cheerfully he seems to
grin,
How neatly spreads his claws,
And welcomes little fishes in
With gently smiling jaws!

Lewis Carroll

Precious stones

An emerald is as green as grass;
A ruby red as blood;
A sapphire shines as blue as
heaven;
A flint lies in the mud.

A diamond is a brilliant stone,
To catch the world's desire;
An opal holds a fiery spark;
But a flint holds fire.

Christina Rossetti

Direction of strokes

If your writing is to look well all the down-strokes must run in the same direction. All the joins between letters must do so too.

Write the word 'Handwriting' twice in your exercise book. Draw lines with your ruler along the down-strokes in the first word, and along the joins in the second word, like this:

Handwriting Handwriting

- Do all the down-strokes run in the same direction?
- Do all the joins run in the same direction?

Unless they do your writing will not look neat and tidy.

Write rows of lines like these very quickly:

Practise writing these words quickly and well. You will find it easier to make the strokes regular if you hold your pencil lightly and sit at your desk correctly:

holiday lullaby daylight filled

- Do all the strokes run in the same direction?

Write the words again but more quickly.
See what happens to the strokes this time.

Write this verse carefully and well:

The Rhinoceros

The Rhino is a homely beast,
For human eyes he's not a
feast,
But you and I will never
know
Why Nature chose to make
him so.

Ogden Nash

Look carefully at each word and letter you have written. Can you find any of these faults?

- Letters too short or too tall
- Letters with their tails too long or too curly
- Badly made joins
- Down-strokes not all in the same direction
- Cross-strokes of f or t in the wrong place
- Dot of an i missed out or in the wrong place
- Wrong spacing between letters, words or lines
- Writing not straight across the page

When you have found what you have done wrong, write the passage again. Try not to make the same mistakes.

Now write the passage very quickly and see if you have made any mistakes.

You must learn to write well but you must also be able to write quickly. Write this poem fairly slowly and very carefully:

A Tickle Rhyme

"Who's that tickling my back?"
said the wall.
"Me," said a small
caterpillar. "I'm learning
to crawl."

Ian Serraillier

Write this poem again but more quickly. Is your writing better or worse this time? Have you done anything wrong? Write the passage again very quickly and see if you make any mistakes.

How quickly can you write? Write this sentence as often as you can in one minute:

Mary had a little lamb.

The number of letters (not words) you have written is your writing speed. Most children of your age can write 50 letters in a minute. Some can write as many as 100. How many can you write? Test your writing speed often. You will need someone with a stopwatch or timer to help you.

Many pages in this book will help you with your writing and your spelling at the same time. As you write each word carefully, say it quietly to yourself and notice the spelling pattern.

The words on this page all have an a in the middle and end with an e. This e is called the Magic or Marker e. It changes the sound of the a:

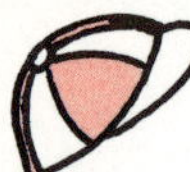 cap becomes cape. 

face race space made trade page

stage cake make wake sale tale

whale became game name lane

escape tape shape date gate late

brave cave gave blaze craze gaze

Write out the passage below carefully and well. Then underline each word which contains the spelling rule taught on this page. How many words did you underline?

The name of the man who won the race into space was Yuri Gagarin and the date was 12 April 1961.

The words on this page all have i in the middle and magic e at the end.

The magic e turns pin into pine.

tribe ice dice nice slice hide

side wife life knife wide bike

like strike mile smile while

time fine line mine pipe ripe

wipe exercise surprise wise

five quite white arrive dive

drive live crime

Write out the passage below carefully and well. Then underline each word which contains the spelling rule taught on this page. How many words did you underline?

His wife told Mike to drive carefully. It is better to arrive late but alive than to crash trying to be on time. That was her wise advice.

These words all have o in the middle and magic e at the end.

The magic e turns  cod into code. 

globe probe robe code rode

strode broke joke smoke hole

pole mole sole dome home Rome

bone cone stone hope Pope

rope slope chose close rose

those note quote vote drove

stove wove doze froze

Write out the passage below carefully and well. Then underline each word which contains the spelling rule taught on this page. How many words did you underline?

The spy strode up and down the slope as he strove to crack the code and drove home to send a note to Rome.

These words all have u in the middle and magic e at the end.

The magic or marker e turns  tub into tube. 

cube tube huge exclude

include rude duke mule rule

yule fortune June prune tune

fuse excuse cute flute mute

Check your writing speed again.
Here is a traditional weather rhyme. See how many times you can copy it in five minutes.

Even though you will be writing quickly your writing must still be readable with all letters and joins properly made. Check your writing against the list of faults on page 10.

Red sky at night
Shepherd's delight.
Red sky in the morning
Shepherd's warning.

chain chalk champion chase
cheap chicken chose church
shady shadow share shelf shoe
shield shop shelter shunt shore
thank thatch theatre then
thief third thought thumb
whale what white whistle

Choose words from the list above to complete these sentences:

1. A _____ stole from a _____
2. A policeman blew his _____ and started to _____ him.
3. A _____ _____ is the hero of the story 'Moby Dick'.

ache machine beech speech

recharge which touch much

such bashful splash fresh

mesh bishop fisher cosh cloth

mushroom pushchair bath

lather path father tether

Choose words from the list above to complete these sentences:

1. The baby's ______ pushed her in her ______

2. Try not to ______ the water in your ______ tonight.

3. In the cathedral the ______ wore his cape made of jewelled ______

a jigsaw puzzle

a box of crackers

a selection box

a Christmas annual

a chess set

a box of paints

a construction set

a computer game

a doll's house

a Cindy doll

a toy garage

an Action Man soldier

a model aeroplane kit

Ingredients: 4 bananas
1 egg white 25 grams caster sugar
150 millilitres of double cream
Method: Mash the bananas to a smooth purée. Whisk the egg white until stiff, then whisk in the sugar. Fold the banana purée and the egg mix into the whipped cream.

Spoon into individual dishes and serve immediately with crisp biscuits.

Serves 4 to 6 people.

blunder blanket blunt block

blade blitz blouse bless bleed

cloak clue clever claim clutter

flesh flake flow float flavour

flush flat flinch flight fleet

glory glen glade glove gleam glide

plenty plough plain plot plan

The cl words have been written in alphabetical order by looking at the third and fourth letter in each word. Copy them out:

claim clever cloak clue clutter

Put the gl and pl words in the list in alphabetical order and copy them into your book.

The fl words have been written in alphabetical order. Copy them into your book:

flake flat flavour fleet flesh

flight flinch float flow flush

Do the same thing for the bl words.

brain brakes bread broken bruise

crashed crew crime crown crumb

grand grease grief grey grumbled

draw driver drown drug drum

trade triangle trap truck trunk

Carefully copy out these sentences and underline all the words taken from the lists above:

The truck driver's leg was broken when the brakes failed and he crashed into a tree trunk.

The hungry crew grumbled because there was no bread left to eat, not even a crumb.

scald scale scan scooter sculpture

skate skeleton sketch skid skin

slate sleep sledge sleeve slide slow

small smart smile smoke smooth

snake snap snarl snort snow

spade spark special sponge spurt

stable stalk steady sting stunt

swam sweater swift swing sword

Copy out these word definitions, together with the word in the list above to which each definition refers:

1. A vehicle on runners instead of wheels for travelling on snow.

2. A carving in wood, metal, stone or clay.

black stack truck deck wreck
brick quick stick clock shock
pluck truck hand stand and
beyond funds under thunder
bang sang length England bring
finger along strong wrong lung

Copy out each of these word definitions, together with the word in the list above to which it refers:

1. The loud noise often heard after a flash of lightning.
2. The part of the human arm beyond the wrist.
3. An instrument for measuring time.

fast past castle best lest fist

history cost lost dust trust

bank plank thank sank drink

sink think donkey monk trunk

pant plant bent sent went

hint mint pint grunt stunt

Copy out each of these word definitions, together with the word in the list above to which it refers:

1. A place where money is coined by stamping metal.

2. A study of past events and the deeds of people.

3. A man who takes a vow to live apart from the world in poverty.

staff cliff coffin offer chaff
coffee toffee bluff cuff stuff
ball fall wall shall spell tell
yellow hill kill still trolley
holly dull full pull brass
class grass dress press kiss
miss boss cross fuss

Copy out each of these word definitions, together with the word in the list above to which it refers:

1. The person in charge.
2. A steep rock-face at the coast.
3. An evergreen shrub with prickly dark green leaves.

Can you guess what these places are?
The capital letters and the shape of the word will help you.

You can see from this how important it is to make capitals well.

Practise writing the capitals as shown on page 2. When you can write them quickly and well, write these words:

Sunday Monday Tuesday
Wednesday Thursday Friday
January February March
April May June July
August September October
November December

Can you write a country for each letter of the alphabet, starting with these:

Australia Belgium Canada

The names of towns also start with capital letters. Can you find a town or city for each letter of the alphabet, starting with these:

Andover Bristol Coventry

People's names also start with capitals. Write the names of the children in your class. Then write their names out again in alphabetical order.

Write this passage very carefully but not too slowly. The spaces between the letters, words and lines must be correct.

Thirty days has September,
April, June and November.
All the rest have thirty-one,
Except February alone,
Which has twenty-eight days
clear,
And twenty-nine in each leap
year.

Check what you have written against the faults list on page 10. Write the passage again more quickly and see what faults there are this time.

This sentence has all the letters of the alphabet in it. Practise writing it very quickly.

The quick brown fox jumps
over the lazy dog.

In each line below there are words from which two letters have been left out. Decide what each word is and write it correctly spelled and correctly joined. You can check your work by looking back at the page numbers indicated.

Page

12 s--ce, b--ame, e--ape, --ave.

13 t--be, sm--e, --ercise, q-it-.

14 gl--e, sm--e, -to-e, v-t-, --oze.

15 c--e, in--ude, d-k-, f--e.

16 ch--n, sh--y, th--k, w--re.

17 ma--ine, t--ch, s--ash, f--her.

20 bla--et, --ever, --avour, fli--t.

21 --ead, cr--n, --and, dr--er.

22 --eleton, sl--p, --ecial, st--dy.

23 w-e-k, q-ic-, st--d, b--ond.

24 ca--le, hi--ory, -ha-k, -onke-.

25 cli--, to--ee, ye--ow, gra--.

Make sure you can write the numerals correctly and quickly:

0 1 2 3 4 5 6 7 8 9

Are all your figures the same size?

Here is a list showing the lengths in miles of some important rivers. Rewrite the list in order of length starting with the shortest. Pay particular attention to your figures.

Amazon 4195, Clyde 106,
Ganges 1500, Murray 1600,
Rhine 800, Mississippi 2350,
Nile 4145, Volga 2325,
Seine 473, Thames 210.

When you set out sums on paper it is important to arrange the rows and columns in straight lines. Copy these sums out carefully and work out the answers:

```
  5029      4051     3129
  4631    - 3672       x 6
+ 7468    ______    ______
______    ______    ______
______
```

151 Abbey Street,
East Town,
Devon WX4 9PW
1 April 1984

Dear John,

I am learning to write quickly and well. When I take the trouble to write a page that looks good I feel proud and want to show people.

Writing quickly will help me with my lessons too.

Yours sincerely,

For a few charmed days
cherry trees flowering now
along the April avenues
gently drop their Japanese
confetti,
pink and white petals
blown by small breezes
on pavements, damp roads,
as if they know that somewhere
there was a spring wedding,
music freely provided
by a glad chorus
of blackbirds and thrushes.

Leonard Clark

When eleven of the fairies had given their gifts, the baby had been promised everything in the world one could wish for.

At that moment, the twelfth fairy suddenly arrived. She was furious because the King had not invited her to the feast. Pointing to the baby, she cried in a loud voice, "When the King's daughter is fifteen years old, she shall prick herself with a spindle and fall down dead."